C000271999

A BOOT UP

BATH

Rodney Legg

First published in Great Britain in 2010

British Library Cataloguing-in-Publication Data
A CIP record for this title is available from the British Library

ISBN 978 1 906887 84 1

PiXZ Books
Halsgrove House, Ryelands Industrial Estate,
Bagley Road, Wellington, Somerset TA21 9PZ
Tel: 01823 653777
Fax: 01823 216796
email: sales@halsgrove.com

An imprint of Halstar Ltd, part of the Halsgrove group of companies
Information on all Halsgrove titles is available at: www.halsgrove.com

Printed and bound in China by Toppan Leefung Printing Ltd

Contents

How to use this book

The area

Roman Bath, like Rome itself, is surrounded by its Seven Hills. These are the obvious target for walks up and out of the city. Inevitably, however, they are somewhat demanding, so walks that are short but strenuous have been mixed with those that are easy but longer. The latter, with circuits up to nine miles, stretch out along the River Avon and its parallel waterscape, the Kennet and Avon Canal. The towpath heads towards creations of industrial archaeology of national renown, such as the Dundas Aqueduct, where canal long-boats cross three other transport systems — rail, river and road.

Scenic and exhilarating country walking is literally within sight and step as you reach out from the city. On one side the skyline becomes the Cotswold Hills, encapsulated at its most civilised in Dyrham Park, whereas on the other side the deep-cut valleys hide some of the most desirable homes in the land, around villages like Combe Hay, Freshford and Southstoke.

Walking is as free and easy as any form of healthy activity. Places are selected with problem-free parking and public houses and tea-rooms en route if possible. Instructions are as basic and clear as possible, but you will also have things to see pointed out to you.

The emphasis throughout is to notice what is odd and quirky - so you do not miss what makes the effort and exercise truly worthwhile.

The routes

With one exception, the routes are circular - meaning they bring you back to your starting point - and are of moderate length. They vary from **two to nine** miles and are graded from one to three boots - from easy to the more challenging. They are ideal for families or groups of friends looking for an afternoon in glorious historic countryside or for a more leisurely walk with a suitable pause at a pub or refreshment spot en route. Little of the terrain is pushchair friendly, so back-pack the toddler.

Starting points are given with map references and postcodes, because the latter are necessary for some car-borne navigation systems, including that used by an ambulance crew who told me they were 15 minutes late arriving at an emergency because no postcode was given.

Direction details specify compass points which, clockwise, are N (north), NNE (north-northeast), NE (north-east), ENE (east-northeast), E (east), ESE (east-southeast), SE (south-east), SSE (south-southeast), S (south), SSW (south-southwest), SW (south-west), WSW (west-southwest), W (west), WNW (west-northwest), NW (north-west) and NNW (north-northwest). The general direction can be assumed to remain the same until another compass point is given. Carry a compass.

Routes are along public rights of way or across access land. Both categories may be subject to change or diversion. Remember that conditions under foot will vary greatly according to the season and weather. Even urban paths can be muddy.

Parking spaces are specified on the assumption that many walkers will arrive by car or bicycle. Public transport options are widely available around the city but check these with the provider before setting off. Ensure you know the time of the last bus or train.

Maps

Though we give a self-contained potted description of each walk you may need a map or global positioning system to find its parking point. Our sketch maps can only be a rough guide. A detailed map will prove useful if you stray away from the route or have to cut the walk short. Phillip's Street Atlas (Bristol & Bath) is excellent.

Bath, as far as the Ordnance Survey is concerned, is covered by Explorer Map 155 (Bristol & Bath). Countryside south of the city appears on Explorer 142 (Shepton Mallet & Frome). Access www.ordnancesurvey.co.uk/leisure for availability.

Key to Symbols Used

Level of difficulty:

Easy 🐾

Fair 🐾 🐾

More challenging 🐾 🐾 🐾

Map symbols:

🚐 Park & start

🚻 WC

— Tarred Road

----- Footpath

■ Building / Town

🍺 Pub

▲ Landmark

+ Church

▪▪▪▪ Railway Line

    River or Stream

— National Trust

Walk Locations

Dyrham
4

A46

3 Batheaston

5

10 A431   **Bath**
9 A36   1   Bathampton
Newton
St Loe   2

6

Southstoke Limpley
8   Stoke 7

A367   A36

1 Roman City and Georgian Bath

A simple 2-mile circuit of the inner city with potential diversions both Roman and Georgian

Bath had the most impressive collection of Roman buildings north of the Alps. They were built across a steaming marsh, from about 90 AD, to utilise geothermal springs. Ice Age melt-waters, snow until 11000 BC, emerge from the Earth's mantle at 47 degrees Celsius (115 degrees Fahrenheit). Aquae Sulis, a 23-acre walled town, was dedicated to the Celtic goddess Sul whose attributes were combined with those of the classical healing deity Minerva, in the temple and spa of Sulis Minerva. Original baths and foundations of the Roman walls, incorporating an extraordinary museum, can now be explored in an underground circuit entered via the Georgian Pump Room beside York Street. The lead-lined Great Bath was discovered in 1881. Our above-ground

Level:
Length: 2 miles
Terrain: Entirely on flat ground through city streets.
Park & start: In Bath and begin the walk from **Bath Spa Station** which is close to the **Broad Quay** crossing of the **River Avon**, reached by the **A367** from Wells and the **A36** from Bristol.
Start ref.: ST 753 643
Postcode: BA1 1SS
Public transport: Bath is the hub for both bus and rail services.
Websites: www.romanbaths.co.uk
www.victoriagal.org.uk

route begins from Bath Spa Station and attempts to follow the line of the Roman and mediaeval walls, from which there are short diversions into the city to see the Roman Baths, Bath Abbey and other historic buildings.

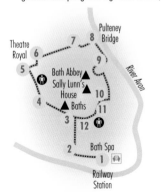

Pulteney Bridge

1 Set off left (W) and walk the length of **Dorchester Street** to its junction opposite the **Post Office** in 250 metres. The Roman bridge over the River Avon was to your left.

2 Turn right (N), away from the main road, into pedestrianised **Southgate Street**. Approach **Stall Street** in 250 metres. This was the site of the Roman South Gate through the Roman wall. The Roman Baths lie straight ahead, in a further 250 metres, being reached via the 1795-rebuilt Pump Room on the corner with York Street.

3 Our onward route turns left (WNW) into **Lower Borough Walls**. The Roman wall was superseded by the mediaeval Bur Walls. Pass the **Lamb and Lion**. To the right, draining into Hot Bath Street, were a rectangular Roman bath and a circular one beyond. Nowhere Lane ran beside Abbey Church House on the site of the Lazars' Hospital.

Gaius Julius Solinus, writing in 230 AD, described a perpetual fire (of Somerset coal) in the temple of Minerva at Bath, which 'never whitens into ash but as the flame fades turns into balls of rock'.

(4) In 500 metres, opposite **Bath College**, we pass between **Westgate Buildings** and **St John's Hospital** (NW) to **Seven Dials** and Monmouth Street on the site of the Roman and mediaeval West Gate in 250 metres. Bear left, between **Sainsbury's Local** and the **Coffee House**, up the hill. St Michael's Church, to the right, served the parish

of St Michael by the Bath. Across to the left, Kingsmead Square lies outside the wall, in what was the fun part of Tudor Bath. To the left of the street was the Fives Court and the Cockpit was on the right.

Beau Nash, Ralph Allen, John Wood the Elder, John Wood the Younger, William Pulteney, Robert Adam and Thomas Baldwin were largely responsible for the creation of Georgian Bath.

(5) Turn right (E) into **St John's Place** in 125 metres. Turn left (N), in 50 metres, into **Trim Street**. The **Theatre Royal** - a Georgian gem - is one of the oldest, most beautiful and active playhouses in the land.

Thermal waters

Sulis Minerva pediment

(6) Turn right (ENE), beside **Gascoyne Place** in 25 metres, into **Upper Borough Walls**. Gascoyne Tower marked the corner of the ancient walls. Timber Green used to be the right, followed by **Bluecoat House** on the site of Roman buildings and the historic Bridewell. There is a section of mediaeval wall opposite the **Royal National Hospital for Rheumatic Diseases**. Roman mosaics, hypocaust and an altar have been discovered beside Union Street.

Theatre Royal

7 Proceed for 500 metres to the junction with **Northgate Street**. This is on the site of North Gate. Turn right, and then immediately left, into **Bridge Street**. The wall passed to the left of St Michael's Church and then turned right in 100 metres through what is now the **Victoria Art Gallery**. This houses the best regional collection of British and European paintings from the 15th century to the present day.

Edgar of Wessex was crowned King of England on 11 May 973 in Bath – which is named 'Acemannesceaster' in the Anglo-Saxon Chronicle – by the Archbishops of Canterbury and York.

8 Approach 1777-dated **Pulteney Bridge**. Turn right (SE) into **Grand Parade** with the **River Avon** and its weirs across to the left. Pass Boat Stall Lane on the site of the Roman East Gate - later called Lod Gate - and the Fish Cross. Ancient buildings were abundant hereabouts. The High Cross, Guildhall (replaced in 1775) and Market House stood in the middle of the High Street, together with the pillory and the stocks.

9 **Orange Green**, facing **Orange Grove** in 300 metres, used to be Mitre Green. This is the ideal point for diverting into the city to visit **Bath Abbey**. Hereon the line of the city wall heads towards the railway (SSE). Bricks, mortar, roads and a little grass cover the former Abbey precincts at Lower Abbey Orchard, the Old Bowling Green, Abbey Gardens, Cloisters, Bagnio, Bishop's Palace and Abbey Gate.

10 Find **No. 4 North Parade Passage**. It is known as **Sally Lunn's House** for the lady who made Bath buns here in 1680. Her successors still hand-bake to the original recipe, for the tea-room, and cook a traditional English trencher dinner each evening. The four-storey building dates from about 1482.

Though Anglo-Saxon in origin, 16th-century Bath Abbey – on the site of the nave of the Norman Cathedral founded by John de Villula – is now the city's parish church of St Peter and St Paul.

11 The precise course of the city wall was between Sally Lunn's and the **Abbey Hotel**. It then passed to the rear of North Parade Buildings. Turn right (S) into **Pierrepont Street** in 100 metres.

Lead-lined Great Bath

John Betjeman lamented the redevelopment of much of the city in the 1960s: 'Goodbye to old Bath. We who loved you are sorry. They've carried you off by the developer's lorry.'

Sally Lunn's House

(12) Turn right (W) in 50 metres into **Pierrepont Place**. Bear left (SW) along **Old Orchard Street** in 75 metres. Pass the Masonic Hall - which was the original Theatre Royal in 1750 - with its plaque for actress Sarah Siddons. Turn right (W) in **Henry Street** in 150 metres. Former Ham Gate was to the right. Continue straight ahead along **New Orchard Street** to return to **Southgate Street** in 300 metres. Both the Bus Station and Bath Spa Station are down to the left in 500 metres. Returning along **Dorchester Street** we cross **Bumditch** culvert - the city's ancient sewer - which incorporates the almost 2,000-year-old sulphurous drain from the Roman Baths. It empties between the bridges into the River Avon.

Baths and Abbey

A 6-mile circuit that goes up and down the hills between stunning follies in the landscape

'Lift up mine eyes unto the hills,' from Bath, at one of the great European skylines. Count the hills, for they are said to have replicated in

Roman minds the Seven Hills of Rome. Those hills were heavily peopled in pre-history, being entrenched with field systems, settlements and hill-forts, though as a backdrop to the neo-classical revival of Georgian Bath they became increasingly wooded. Today there are almost too many trees, such as around the Sham Castle eye-catcher, which is of national significance as it was built by the most notable of folly designers - Sanderson Miller - in 1762. His commission was from Ralph Allen who introduced John Wood to Bath, and was its Postmaster. He proved that Bath's own cream lime-

Level:
Length: 6 miles
Terrain: Mostly clear well-used paths but some across undulating rough ground.
Park & start: From the layby on the south side of **Claverton Down Road** between the **Norwood Avenue** turning into the University and the entrance to **Rainbow Wood Farm**.
Start ref.: ST 774 638
Postcode: BA2 7AR
Public transport: Buses to University.
Websites: www.americanmuseum.org.uk
www.nationaltrust.org.uk

stone could do for the city what Portland Stone had done for London. Folly-styled Prior Park landscape, the American Museum in Claverton Park, and the time-warp perfection of Widcombe are also en route.

1 Set off by crossing to the pavement on the other side of the road (SE) and head away from the University and the farm for 400 metres. Pass **Fieldways Lodge** and **The Hollies** and re-cross the road to a kissing gate to the left of a field gate. Further left are **Bramley Cottages** with apple trees on the roadside grass.

2 A public path heads (S) into National Trust land through a corridor of fences with Rainbow Wood Farm to the right and **Claverton Down** across the stone wall to the left. After the third kissing gate the wall approaches houses to the left and trees to the right.

City view

3 On reaching the houses in 500 metres we turn right (SW) into the wood. On reaching an old quarry the path turns left, in 150 metres, across a stone stile, to the right of a house. Enter the field beyond its garden. Keep the wood to

the right for 300 metres and the uninspiring lines of **Ralph Allen School** to the left. Ahead is the more stylish 1906-built Bath Clinic modern extensions. Cross the stile between the school and the clinic.

Claverton Down

4 Turn right (W) along the road, beside the clinic and the entrance to **Combe Grove Manor Hotel**. Much quarried **Fairy Wood**, owned by the National Trust, is to the right and **Paddock Wood** to the left.

5 Turn right (NNE) in 400 metres, after **Klondike House** entrance, through the next gate. This entrance, into **Rainbow Woods**, is opposite the junction with **Shaft Road**. Follow the main path straight ahead between two blocks of woodland. Bear left (NW) in 200 metres, to enter the sports pitches of **Monument Field**, and cross them diagonally towards the centre of Bath. Cross the stile beside the gate on the other side, into the trees in 300 metres, and emerge to a stunning view of the city.

6 Cross the stile beside the left-hand gate and go down the slope towards Bath. Pass to the right of a solitary hillside ash tree and then to the left of the gate. Descend along the spur of the hill towards the woodland surrounding the lakes. Klondike House overlooks the valley from the right in an assertive echo in golden stone of the discovery made in Canada's far west on 16 August 1896.

7 On reaching the boundary of **Prior Park** we turn right (N) and keep the landscape gardens to the left. You have a perfect glimpse of the Paladian bridge above the waterfall between the lakes. The path becomes **Church Lane** on passing **The Dell** in 200 metres.

Prior Park

Prior Park House, with its Corinthian frontage of 1,300 feet to John Wood's designs, became a 'comfortless palace' for the Catholic College of Saints Peter and Paul.

8 Climb up into **Widcombe** in 300 metres, to **St Thomas Becket Church** and the elegant perfection of **Widcombe Manor**.

9 Turn right (NE) into **Church Street** and then right (E) at the cross-roads in 200 metres. Cross to the left-hand pavement to climb **Widcombe Hill**. Spot the '1 Mile from the Guildhall, Bath' plaque and stone beside **Greenlea**. National Trust land begins on the left after the bulging wall of **Winfarthing**.

The 'Lower Grounds' at Prior Park were given to the National Trust by the Catholic Brothers and Prior Park College in 1993.

10 Turn left (NW) into it, across the stile to the left of the field gate, opposite **Prospect Road** junction. Then turn left again, across a stile beside the next gate, down across the field below Winfarthing, towards

Bath Abbey and the old Imperial Hotel. There is a stile in the hedgerow in front of the hotel - now a theatre - in 300 metres.

Widcombe Manor

11 Turn right (NE) to exit from Trust land beside the burial ground in 150 metres. Continue into the drive beside **Smallcombe Farm** and then straight ahead up the narrow path between the hedges. Pass more National Trust land and continue into the next batch of skyline woods in 400 metres. Here we emerge at a kissing gate between **Hill Coach House** and Little Claverton.

Sham Castle (back view)

Smallcombe

12 Turn right (SE) up **Bathwick Hill**. Turn left (N) in 600 metres, beside the letterbox after **Cedar Lodge**, into **North Lane** which is opposite **Woodland Place**. Turn left (NW) in 50 metres. Pass **Quarry Road** in 100 metres. Turn right in a further 50 metres, after the drive to **Woodside House**, to a stile and the field beside National Trust woods.

13 Pass the **Sham Castle** in 500 metres and proceed straight ahead (N), between yet more National Trust woodland and the **Golf Club** buildings. Then pass to the right of the gate adjoining a galvanised building. Cross the stile to the left of a transformer pole and follow the track to the communications mast compound in 700 metres.

The Prior Park landscape, is one of Lancelot 'Capability' Brown's gems, polished with advice from satirist Alexander Pope and inspiration from manic-depressive poet William Shenstone.

14 Initially bear left (NE) above **The Trossachs** with Bathampton down to the left and the golf course fence to the right. Gradually bear right (ENE) across the banks of prehistoric fields. Iron Age Bathampton Camp is up to the right. Keep to this contour, with trees and scrub to the left, for 600 metres. Join a hollow way and look out for a marker post in the brambles.

15 Turn right here (ESE), uphill into the wood, and stay on the main track which becomes increasingly rocky. Cross a stile in 300 metres and turn right (SW) ignoring the signed skyline walk. Ours is the path directly up the slope, which is paved with grooved stones of an incline-operated tramway, constructed in the early 19th century for lowering quarry stone.

16 Turn left (S) at the top, in 100 metres, through the workings and scrubby woodland. Turn right beside **The Rock** and pass to the right of a quarry shaft. Turn left (SE) at the plateau in 300 metres. This is a permissive path with woods to the left and the fairways to the right.

Ralph Allen's Prior Park provided the 'Allworthy' for Tom Jones – the first English novel – which was being written by Henry Fielding at Twerton.

17 Turn left at the end of the golf course (NE), down into the woods, and then right (SE) in 50 metres. This returns us to the way-marked skyline route, through National Trust parkland (S) at **Bushey Norwood**. The **University Campus** is across to the right. Pass an alignment of modern-day stones. Beyond them, at the stone wall in 600 metres, we cross a stile into another National Trust field.

18 Turn right, over to the corner and a track through the trees to the road in 150 metres. Woodland to the left conceals Claverton Manor and the American Museum (entrance downhill in 150 metres). Our walk goes the other way (W), uphill, towards the sounds of an **RSPCA Rescue Centre**. Turn left (S) in 150 metres, across a stile, and follow the hedge with an arable field to the left and the animals to the right. From the end of the field in 300 metres we follow the wall of **The Hollies**. Turn right (W) to your car in a further 300 metres.

Built by Ralph Allen in 1762, the skyline Sham Castle folly was restored and presented to the city of Bath, in 1921.

3 Batheaston and Swainswick

A 5-mile circuit with historic villages,
wartime aviation relics and classic views

Level: 🥾 🥾
Length: 5 miles
Terrain: Good paths but several steep slopes, both up and down, as the penalty for the views.
Park & start: Roadside parking at **St John the Baptist Church** in **Batheaston** on approaching **Northend** suburb from the A4.
Start ref.: ST 778 679
Postcode: BA1 7EF
Public Transport: Bus to Batheaston.
Websites: www.batheastonchurches.org.uk
www.swainswickchurch.org.uk

From Little Solsbury Hill and Charmy Down we have classic views. Little Solsbury, named for its stoutly-built Iron Age fort and settlement, is one of the city's Seven Hills. Folklore links Solsbury

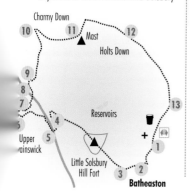

with a temple of Apollo, built by Bladud, the legendary Druidic ruler 'who tried to fly'. Bath is beautiful and even the add-on modern extras look acceptable from a distance. We visit the ancient parish churches of Batheaston and Swainswick. That's a romantic name - Danish merged with Anglo-Saxon - meaning swain's dairy farm. A swain was a rustic likely lad; the youthful lover in pastoral poetry. The time-warp includes a wartime fighter aerodrome, across a wide plateau at 690-feet on the southern flank of the Cotswold Hills. Whether you find it equally charming is in the eye of the

beholder. Unlike so many other airfields, it has reverted to limestone downland rather than intensive agriculture or housing estates. It has become an oasis of wild flowers and bird song.

Batheaston Church

2 Turn right (W), continuing up the hill, up **Solsbury Lane**. Turn right (NW) at the road junction in 400 metres, for a stiff climb for a further 400 metres, and enter National Trust land at the top. Proceed up and over skyline hummocks of Iron Age fortifications that encircle **Little Solsbury Hill**. The plateau rampart, faced with drystone walling, has one of the classic views of Bath and Batheaston, plus the Avon valley and parts of four counties.

Little Solsbury features in a verse by Alexander Pope, based on its King Bladud associations: 'Then shall thy Solsbury echo with thy name, and ev'ry babe shall lisp Apollo's fame.'

1 Set off (SW) from the **Church Lane** junction with your back to the parish church, up the steps, opposite **Glebe Cottage**, following the sign for Bailbrook. Enter the field and follow the hedge, and do likewise in the next pasture - keeping it to your left - uphill to the **Telephone Exchange** and the road facing **Hill Farm Flats** in 300 metres.

3 Continue straight ahead for 500 metres, across the summit and downhill, towards the sight and sound of traffic on Gloucester Road. Exit from the downland across a stile in the scrub into the top right-hand corner of the field above Upper Swainswick. Follow the dense hedgerow down into the valley, keeping it to your right and the farm and A46 across to the left.

Little Solsbury

Puritan pamphleteer William Prynne (1600-69) who bravely bore Star Chamber disfigurements – his ears cut off and cheeks branded 'SL' for 'Seditous Libeller' (or 'Stigmata Laudis' as he defiantly put it) – is buried at Swainswick.

4 As we converge with the highway, in 700 metres, there is a three-way path junction. Turn left here (SW), for 50 metres, to the field gate in front of the conifers of **Homefield**. Turn left (S), down the drive, and then follow the slip road to the left, around the bend and under the main road in 350 metres.

Swainswick Church is a marvellous architectural mix from Norman times onwards, including effigies and the graves of architects John Wood the elder and John Wood the younger from Bath.

5 Then turn right (N), up beside the former garage, and turn left (NW) in 250 metres into **Upper Swainswick**. Enter the village beside **Limberlost** and proceed straight ahead for 200 metres. Turn downhill, beside **Upper Swainswick House**, at the oak tree on the green. Then turn left, in 100 metres, beside the floral wall at **The Batch**, down a cobbled pavement to **Glebe House** and the cemetery.

6 Take the penultimate turning on the right, between the churchyard and the cemetery, with a perfect view of **St Mary's Church**. Then turn right at the next junction, beside the archetypal **Manor House**, framed by a great copper beech. We are now heading uphill and turn right in just 20 metres. This 400 metre circuit of the historic village returns us to The Batch.

7 Instead of re-passing the cottages we turn left (N) between **Naille** and **Lansdown View**. Climb **Kent Lane**, which becomes a deep-cut track beneath a tunnel of vegetation, to **Blacksmith Lane** and the old course of **Gloucester Road** in 250 metres.

8 Here we turn left and then right to the verge of the new highway. Cross with care, to the layby, if it is safe to do so. Should congestion make this unwise, follow the road down to the underpass, and then walk uphill on the other side.

9 Cross the upper of the two stiles, beside the slip-road, rather than the layby proper. Head uphill towards the scrubby flora-rich limestone grassland with Bath behind you. Turn right in 200 metres, through a gap in the hawthorn, and continue up the slope to the fence in 100 metres. Cross the stile and bear right, following the boundary around two sides of the field, and go through the gap in the stone wall in 400 metres. Bear right into the tongue of grassland above the wood in 300 metres.

St Mary's churchyard

10 Turn left along the lane and then left across the stile under the ash tree in 15 metres. In 350 metres, having passed a brick-built generator house on the edge of wartime **RAF Charmy Down** we turn right (E) across a stile. Then bear right (SE) over what is now a great nesting ground for skylark and lapwing. Pass the horseshoe-shaped blast wall of an aeroplane dispersal pad. Go through the gate and follow the taxi-way (E)

RAF Charmy Down became operational in December 1940, with the arrival of the Hurricanes of 87 Squadron, under 10 Group Fighter Command which had its headquarters four miles away at Box.

to the communications mast. Ignore other paths to the left and right. The line of concrete cupola observation slits are above the underground head-quarters rooms.

11 Proceed straight ahead, from the mast, along the central option (NE). Then turn right (ESE) in 250 metres. Leave the aerodrome and pass to the right of the remains of a wartime hutted encampment. At the end of the two fields, in 500 metres, we enter a double-walled unpaved road and descend across **Holts Down** (SE).

RAF Charmy Down

12 Continue straight ahead, down an asphalt road, in 500 metres. Also go straight on, downhill, at a cross-roads in a further 750 metres (S). This is **Hollies Lane** and we re-enter Batheaston on **The Hill** in 300 metres.

Swainswick Manor

13 Turn right (SE) in 300 metres and pass **Pound Hill House**. Further down, on the left, is the pound itself which was restored by the Batheaston Society in 1973. Admire the eagle surmounting 1729-dated **Eagle House** in 250 metres. Proceed through the village, via the **Northend Inn**, to the parish church in a further 500 metres.

4 West Littleton and Dyrham

Reaching the Cotswold Way in a 6-mile circuit of Dyrham Park

The best parkland in the southern folds of the Cotswold Hills, between Bath and the motorway, is at Dyrham. The National Trust cares for a composite

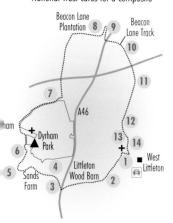

historic landscape. Chatting with the rector, Revd Victor Howlett, I was reminded that despite appearances his church does not belong to the Trust and is the oldest integral part of the scene. Standing on a wall, it overlooks the Dutch-style mansion of Dyrham House and its setting of 'modest grandeur' which was created between 1691 and 1702 by William Blathwayt - who was William III's War Secretary and Secretary of State, with a Great Hall from Tudor times preserved at its centre. Dyrham Park can be visited if it is open and you have the time. West Littleton is totally unlike Dyrham. It

Level: ♥ ♥
Length: 6 miles
Terrain: Well-marked paths, easy to follow, but with a few quite steep slopes.
Park & start: Beside the village green in **West Littleton** which is reached by turning east from the A46 a mile south of Tormarton Interchange (Junction 18 on the M4).
Map ref.: ST 761 755
Postcode: SN14 8ER
Public transport: Buses from Bath to Stroud.
Websites: www.dyrham-village-hall.com
www.nationaltrust.org.uk

surrounds a village green high on the hills. Home Farm is placed near the middle and another four farms are at each corner of the village envelope. These are Church Farm, Manor Farm, West Farm and Upper Farm.

25

1 Set off along the path through the churchyard (W) in 150 metres. Cross a stile on the other side and go through the copse beside the equestrian exercise area for 50 metres. Bear right in the field and cross it to the wooden gate in the stone wall in 150 metres.

Dyrham House and contents were handed to the National Trust by the Treasury, after being accepted in lieu of death duties in 1956, with the 274-acres of grounds and parkland being acquired in 1976.

Inner courtyard, Dyrham House

St Peter's Church has its own treasures including life-size brasses of Sir Morys Russel and Lady Isabel Russel – dating from 1401 and 1415 – and effigies of George Wynter (died 1588) and wife Anne in a huge sculpture.

2 Proceed for just 20 metres but do not cross the stepped stile over the next wall. Instead turn left (SW), through a hunting gate, and follow the walls and hedges along the rim of the valley, for 1,200 metres. Pass to the left of **Littleton Wood Barn**. In 300 metres, to the left of the oaks of **Littleton Wood**, we cross the stone stile beside the gate.

3 Turn right (NW) down the road to the staggered cross-roads in 100 metres. Cross with care to the road to Dyrham village. Follow the wall of Dyrham Park down to the second gate in 175 metres.

4 Turn left directly opposite, across a stile, beside the field gate. Go along the farm track (WNW) and follow the stone wall towards the view of Bristol and the Welsh valleys. In 600 metres, above **Sands Farm**,

bear left (W) for the steep descent. Cross the farm drive in 150 metres and continue to the bottom of the field in a further 200 metres.

1698-dated stables

Garden cascade

5 Turn right (N) along the Cotswold Way, keeping the field boundary to the left, to a kissing gate above **Dyrham** village. Turn left (NW), down **Sands Hill**, and pass between **Grove Cottage** and **Poplar Lodge**. Turn right (N) beside **Dyrham Cottage** in 150 metres. On approaching the next corner in 300 metres we have a view into the grounds of **Dyrham House** with **St Peter's Church** set on the wall beside it. From the corner it is a diversion of 200 metres to see the church. Excavations in the grass reveal paths from William Blathwayt's famed water gardens which were created in the 1690s.

6 Our onward route from the roadside gate is to fork right (WNW), going behind the wall, along a narrow path flagged with stones, to a gate opposite **Boyd Brook House** in 200 metres. Rejoin the Cotswold Way and turn right (N), up the stony track, to gates and pastures in 150 metres. From here we follow the wall of **Dyrham Park** (NE). Keep it to your right for 1,100 metres. Across the deep-cut valley to the left are the banks of an Iron Age fort on Hinton Hill. The slope beside you is terraced with mediaeval cultivation strips. Views are over Hinton hamlet to Chepstow and the Black Mountains and across Talbot Farm to Pucklechurch village.

Hinton Hill

7 On reaching the barns at **Badminton Plantation** we go through a gate and then turn left (N) along **Field Lane**. Turn left and then immediately right at the junction in 375 metres. Follow the bridleway, keeping the hedge to your left, and pass under the power line.

8 In 900 metres, on approaching the **M4**, bear right (E) and pass a reservoir. Keep the motorway across to your left and follow the path beside **Beacon Lane Wood** into a corner of the field in 600 metres.

9 Go around the corner and then turn right, through a gap in the trees, to the car-park of **Tormarton Interchange** picnic area in 100 metres. Pass the toilet block.

Continue straight ahead through the roadside trees to the pavement beside the **A46** in 75 yards.

10 Turn right (S) for 100 metres. Then cross the busy road (E) to the safety of double-hedged **Beacon Lane**. Follow this green lane for 400 metres, and then the field boundaries (SE) to the electricity pylons in another 600 metres. Cross the road.

Dyrham House

11 Continue straight ahead and join **Wallsend Lane** on the other side of the field. Turn right (S) and follow this track to the brow of the hill between a wartime bunker and a barn in 600 metres. The double-hedged lane descends to **Dunsdown Lane** in another 200 metres.

12 Turn left (S) along the road and pass **Butts End**. Proceed to the next corner in 250 metres. Turn right into a green lane and then left in just 15 metres.

A statue of Neptune looks down from above Dyrham House to the estuary that was romantically known as the Severn Sea.

Dyrham means 'Deer meadow' and the fallow deer grazing its walled parkland are one of the country's oldest herds.

13 Bear right (SW) in the field, up the slope, to the corner in the hedgerow in 100 metres. Follow the hedgerow (S) to the corner of the field in 300 metres.

West Littleton

14 Turn left (E), over the stepped stile, to re-trace your earlier steps back into **West Littleton** in 300 metres.

Around the inner courtyard at Dyrham House, to provide the social fabric to imposing family rooms, the National Trust restored and opened the domestic and servants' quarters of the Blathwayts in 2000.

5 **Bathampton and Batheaston**

*Canal towpath and riverside routes linked
in a 5-mile circuit via Bathampton Down*

Many who were anything in Georgian, Regency and Victorian Bath had Bathampton or Batheaston addresses. They ranged from 'Father of Australia' Admiral Arthur Phillip, old soldiers Lieutenant-General Sir Thomas Dallas

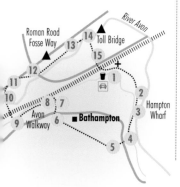

and General Sir Alexander Mackenzie, to geologist Sir Roderick Impey Murchison. A later arrival was the English impressionist painter Walter Sickert. Bathampton is separated from both Batheaston and Bath by an historic transport corridor of canal, river, railway and road. They share a green wedge of lush landscape. The environmental contribution, in combination, is to contain and restrict suburban expansion. Our walk is along the canal towpath for the outward section of the route and the northern return is across riverside meadows. The George Inn has its moorings beside the Kennet and

Level: 🥾
Length: 5 miles
Terrain: Level paths in both sets of meadows but with a big hill to separate them.
Park & start: In **Bathampton**, either in the **High Street** or over the canal bridge in **Tyning Road**.
Start ref.: ST 778 665
Post code: BA2 6TQ
Public transport: Buses from Bathampton.
Websites: www.bathampton-village.org.uk
www.oldmillbath.co.uk

Avon Canal and the River Avon can answer in terms of picturesque hospitality with the Water Wheel Restaurant overlooking a weir and mill-pool. There is a functioning toll barrier on the crossing at Batheaston Bridge.

Bathampton and Batheaston

5

George Inn

(3) The tramway has lost its bridge so we must descend to the main road in 300 metres. Turn left (S) along the verge, downhill, for 150 metres. Cross to a woodland track which climbs to the right (N) as a terrace parallel to the road. Beware of the precipice down to the right. In 150 metres we go under a tramway bridge.

(1) Set off along the canal bank (E) in front of **Bathampton Primary School** - with the bridge behind you - and proceed along the towpath for 1,000 metres to the swing-bridge beside **Old Canal Cottage** at **Hampton Wharf**.

(2) Cross to the opposite bank, below the house, and turn left. Proceed beside the wharf for 80 metres and then turn right (SW), up the slope, and cross a stile. Climb the incline course of a 19th-century tramway which brought stone down to the canal from hilltop quarries.

12th-century sculpture

4 Double back to the right and then cross over the bridge (SW) to resume following the track-bed uphill through **Bathampton Wood**. Stone sleepers were set a yard apart and the railway was cable-operated with loaded trucks descending hauling the empty ones back to the top.

5 Proceed for 600 metres, to a point 100 metres below the summit, and cross a stile. Drop down (NW) into the quarrylands, for 800 metres, and emerge on limestone downland below the grassy ramparts of **Bathampton Camp**. The view is of Lambridge, Batheaston and Bathford (with the church tower).

6 Proceed straight ahead, aiming for the left-hand extremity of the Avon valley - and Bath - with a low bank to your right. Descend across scrubby hummocks of **The Trossachs**. Keep the hilltop to your left. The path becomes a stony track and emerges in 500 metres beside **Bath Corporation Waterworks** and **Warminster Road**, at **St George's Hill** (home of Walter Sickert who died in 1942).

The 12th-century effigy of a praying figure with a chasuble in a niche at Bathampton Church – the oldest ecclesiastical sculpture in Somerset – probably came from Bath Abbey.

Batheaston weirs

7 Cross to **Bathampton Lane** (NE). Descend for 200 metres to **Meadow Lane**, a passageway, between **West House** and **Hessle House**. Turn left (NW), down beside **Meadow View** and **Meadow Croft**, to cross the canal in 200 metres.

8 Turn left (SW), just before the railway bridge, to follow the towpath. Keep the **Kennet and Avon Canal** to your left. Pass footpath bridge **No. 185** in 700 metres. In a further 150 metres, before reaching the bend in the waterway, you come to an ash tree.

9 Turn sharply right (NE) with a paddock to the left and the canal bank to the right. The track descends to a railway bridge in 200

River Avon

metres. Turn left (N) and cross the **River Avon** in 100 metres. Originally built in 1820, **Grosvenor Bridge** was rebuilt a century later, in 1929.

Viscount John Baptise Du Barry went up on to Bathampton Down for a duel and came down dead, in 1778, to be laid out in the old George Inn.

10 Turn right on the other side and then left in 50 metres. Follow **Grosvenor Bridge Road** to the eastern end of five-storey **Grosvenor Lodge** and **Grosvenor Terrace** in 250 metres.

(11) Turn right (E), along the main road - which is the Roman Fosse Way - to pass **Lambridge Training Ground** and the **Lambridge Harvester**. In 250 metres we pass the junction with the former main road up into the Cotswold Hills. Proceed along the **A4**, towards Batheaston and London, uphill for 200 metres to beyond the 1896-dated granite horse-trough. Look out for the gap on the right immediately after the drive to the **Old Barn** and **Lambridge House**.

Passengers are again being carried on the Canal Bus between Bath and Bradford on Avon, and by leisure traffic on the River Avon, where people-carrying craft date back to the 1720s.

(12) Turn right here, and then left in just 5 metres, to pass through a cast-iron stile. Enter a passage between a hedge and a wall, leading (E) to the river and motor-way-style multiple bridges in 500 metres. Here we join a cycleway with the river to the right. After the final span, 15 metres behind it, we turn right (NE) and pass to the right of a sports field.

Hampton Wharf

(13) In 500 metres, after the final pitch, go straight ahead across a stile between two gates. The tracks brings us to the far side of a pasture opposite a mill, where we turn left and then right, in 10 metres. Emerge in 100 metres from a narrow tunnel into the drive of **Old Mill Hotel**.

Scottish engineer John Rennie's Kennet and Avon Canal received its enabling legislation in 1794 and took 16 years to build, westwards across 57 miles of challenging countryside, from Newbury to Bath.

14 Turn left and then right, around and beside the **Toll Point** of **Batheaston Bridge**, in 50 metres. 'Persons walking' are on the board at an uncollectable half-penny a crossing. So watch the motorist pay and go free (S) to the **Water Wheel Restaurant** and **Old Mill Hotel** on the other side.

15 In 500 metres **Tollbridge Road** re-crosses **Batheaston Bypass** - this time looking down on it - and then the railway, ditto. In 150 metres we are back in the village between the 1828-dated **George Inn** and **St Nicholas Church**. 'Parish churches are not museums,' says the church guide, which goes on to prove that this is an exception.

Batheaston Bridge

6 Dundas Aqueduct and Claverton

A linear walk - of optional length - along the most impressive section of the Kennet and Avon Canal

Four miles is the suggested length for this walk but it can be stretched or shrunken to fit your requirements. The

Kennet and Avon Canal joins Bath and Reading, and therefore Bristol to London, and also the Atlantic Ocean with the North Sea. In theory, this could become a circular walk as there is an excellent footpath across meadows beside the River Avon but a linking right of way lacks a bridge. Even without the circuit, there are historical and visual distractions in all directions, including outworks that enabled builder John Rennie to ensure that his canal held water. Variable geology caused catastrophic leakage. The mix of rock, clay and fuller's earth 'worked serious

Level:

Length: 4 miles plus options (choose when to turn back).

Terrain: Benign, being almost entirely along the canal towpath, though diversions involve slopes.

Park & start: In the long layby beside **Warminster Road** - the **A36** - next to R. W. Humpries's garage on the Bath side of the Viaduct Hotel traffic lights at **Monkton Combe**.

Start ref.: ST 783 624

Postcode: BA2 7JD

Public transport: Bus to Limpley Stoke.

Websites: www.british-waterways.co.uk
www.katrust.org.uk

mischief' after heavy rain when the canal slid down into the river. Hidden culverts and tunnels prevent repetition.

37

① Set off (E) from the Bath end of the layby where steps descend beside the electrical **Aqueduct Switching Station**. Turn left at the bottom, in 100 metres, and then right on approaching the stone warehouse and crane (made by Acramans of Bristol) at **Dundas Wharf**. Keep **Dundas Basin** to your left and the lesser channel of the 1801-dated **Somerset Coal Canal**, leading to **Brassknocker Wharf**, to the right.

Boat birds

② In 50 metres the main path crosses the Bath to Westbury branch of the Great Western Railway. Then, in a further 50 metres, we cross one of Britain's finest engineering treasures, namely **Dundas Aqueduct** which carries the **Kennet and Avon Canal** over the **River Avon**.

Dundas Aqueduct (canal above)

3 Follow the canal around the corner, for 150 metres, to see the attractive stretch between an old gate-cottage and **Conkwell Wood**, but then turn back to Dundas Wharf as there is no suitable path circuit on this Wiltshire side of the county boundary.

4 Having returned to the wharf we turn right (N), towards Claverton, and then right in 50 metres to cross bridge **No. 177**. The towpath now follows the right-hand bank. Pass swing-bridge **No. 178**, in 600 metres, and then some elaborate industrial archaeology on the opposite bank. These form part of flood-relief precautions..

5 In 1,000 metres, on reaching road bridge **No. 180** at **Claverton Pumping Station**, we have options. Claverton village is up the slope to the left (SW) in 500 metres. Or you can continue (NE) towards Bath for another stretch of canal towpath. Start to turn back before becoming tired.

St Mary's Church, Claverton, has the pyramidal tomb of Prior Park creator Ralph Allen who was a friend of Alexander Pope and Henry Fielding (and appears in Tom Jones *as Squire Allworthy).*

Designed by John Rennie, Dundas Aqueduct opened in 1805, and is regarded as his seminal achievement in combining engineering and architectural skills.

The towpath

6 The third choice, which I found compelling, is to turn right (NE), and descend along the road for 100 metres to the cottage which lost its front porch to the railway (literally, as trains pass the window at eye-level). 'Step, Look, Listen - Beware of trains.' Listening is particularly important as the line quickly bends out of sight in both directions. Then cross the bridge beside **Pumping Station Pool** and enter the field.

7 Bear right (SE), to cross the meadows for 100 metres, towards Sheephouse Farm and the magnificent curving weirs. Downstream from them the public footpath reaches the river. If, as at the time of writing, there is no bridge in sight, we must turn around and re-trace our steps along the canal to **Dundas Wharf**.

8 Should a bridge have magically appeared, you can walk up to the road, turn right, and then right again through **Sheephouse Farm**. A public path (SW) follows the east bank of the River Avon, below **Warleigh Wood**, to return to the canal towpath on the left side of **Dundas Aqueduct**.

9 If it is any consolation, returning via the towpath (S) - the way we came - is far more dramatic from this direction. You appreciate the full grandeur and magnificence of the aqueduct. In 1951 it became the first British canal relic to be scheduled as an ancient monument.

Dundas Basin

7 Freshford and Monkton Combe

A 6-mile circuit with three attractive villages overlooking the canal and river

Much used to go on in the Avon valley as it twists from Wiltshire into Somerset. There are multiple waterways and railways and other signs of industrial

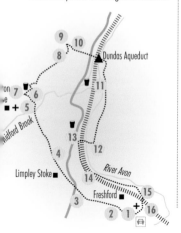

Level: 🥾 🥾
Length: 6 miles
Terrain: Easy, apart from one climb.
Park & start: In **Freshford** village which is reached by turning south-east from the A36 at Limpley Stoke.
Start ref.: ST 789 602
Postcode: BA3 6BX
Public transport: Bus to Freshford.
Websites: www.freshfordsomerset.co.uk
www.monktoncombe.com

activity such as Victorian flock mills at Freshford. The next village has Monkton Combe School as its principal business in the area's second valley that extends sideways from Limpley Stoke. Here the Midford Brook and its network of a canal, railway and roads were the gateway into the Somerset Coalfield which operated from early in Roman times through to the 1970s. Writers and travellers from John Leland and William Camden to John Selden and Richard Pococke referred to coal pits and their 'mineral-mountains' which seems a romantic term for slag heaps. Most of the mining relics have gone, both in the coalfield and the under-

ground Combe Down quarries, which produced much of the honey-coloured stone for Georgian and Regency Bath. The great exception to this story of loss, as we saw in the last walk, is that the Kennet and Avon Canal not only survives but flourishes.

Monkton Combe Lock-up

1 Set off (NW) from **St Peter's Church**, downhill, into the superb panoramic view. The church-yard has the best view in the village. Pass the **Old Parsonage** and turn left (SW), beside **Avondale**, in 150 metres. Turn right (NW) beside **Spring Cottage**, in 50 metres, to climb **Dark Lane**.

Built on the site of a pear tree, St Mary's Church is the sole survivor of seven Anglo-Saxon churches that marked the boundary of the Shaftesbury Abbey estate, and retains an original doorway and arch.

During cold winters when both canals were in use, through the first half of the 19th century, they provided 17 miles of ice-rink for the boys of Downside School to skate into Bath.

2 Turn right in 150 metres, up **Church Lane**, towards Bath. The 'Freshford Slow' sign of the Southern Automobile Club is opposite **Hillside Farm**. Midway up the hill, visit Anglo-Saxon **St Mary's Church** at **Middle Stoke**, beside a junction in 600 metres.

3 Continue along the uphill road. Cross **Warminster Road**, in 350 metres, into **Midford Lane**. Also continue straight ahead beside the entrance to Bath Stone Company's **Stoke Hill Mine**.

Somerset Coal Canal

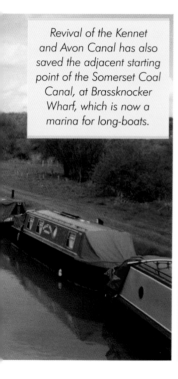

Revival of the Kennet and Avon Canal has also saved the adjacent starting point of the Somerset Coal Canal, at Brassknocker Wharf, which is now a marina for long-boats.

(4) In 500 metres, opposite **Uplands Close**, we turn right (NNW) into the **Old Track**. Continue straight ahead beside **Chatleys**, to the left of the bungalow, in 150 metres. A double-fenced path between fields drops down (NW) into a gully and descends to an unpaved road in 500 metres. Turn right along it (NE) for just 20 metres and then turn left (NW) into another narrow track to descend to the sound of weirs at **Midford Brook** in 250 metres. Cross the water and proceed (N) between the fields to **Monkton Combe Mill** in 150 metres.

(5) Turn left (NW) along **Mill Lane**, into **Monkton Combe**, and cross the course of the branch railway line immortalised by an Ealing Comedy, *The Titfield Thunderbolt*. Pass **Littledale** and **Aprildale**, followed by **Station Cottage**, to a 1776-built **Lock-up** which completes a 300-metre climb up the village street.

(6) Turn left (SW), beside the **Wheelwright's Arms**, to **St Michael's Church** in 100 metres. The present building dates from 1865 but next-door **Monk's Rest** is much older.

(7) Turn right (N) as you face the church, and then right again (NW), in 50 metres. Climb the slope, beside **Fox Cottage**, along a steep path between stone walls. Turn right (E) on reaching the road in 350 metres. Pass **Prospect Cottage** and descend for 600 metres, to a corner opposite **Eddystone** and beside **Bryans**, which is the Headmaster's House of Monkton Combe School.

8 Turn left (NE) into the asphalt road but continue straight ahead as it bends to the left in 100 metres. Go through the kissing gate in the hedge. Cross the hillside pasture, keeping the woods up to the left, to a stile to the left of the crab apple and sycamore in 300 metres. Cross this and enter the lower edge of the wood, through a kissing gate in 200 metres. In 75 metres we emerge on a busy road.

9 Turn left (N), uphill, and cross to walk towards oncoming traffic. Pass **Combe Hill House**, to **Brassknocker Hill Cottages**, in 150 metres. Proceed beyond them, and **Combe Grove Manor**, for 50 metres.

Dundas Aqueduct (from above)

10 Turn right (SE) opposite **Combe Edge House**, over a stone stile beside the 1827-dated cast-iron milestone for Bath Turnpike Trust. Enter a hillside pasture in 150 metres. Keep Claverton Wood and the hedgerow to your left. Descend to the **Warminster Road** in 350 metres.

11 Cross with care to the left-hand end of the long layby. Go down steps to the right of **Aqueduct Pumping Station** and turn left at the bottom, in 100 metres, to approach the warehouse and crane beside **Dundas Basin**. Turn left, keeping the **Kennet and Avon Canal** to the left, with the lesser **Somerset Coal Canal** branching off to the right. Cross **Dundas Aqueduct** in 100 metres. Divert down steps, immediately after it, to appreciate the full architectural splendour from the **River Avon**.

12 Follow the towpath around the corner (S), beside a canal cottage opposite **Conkwell Wood**, and proceed to bridge **No. 175** in 1,500 metres. Join the road opposite the entrance to **Timothy Rise Farm**.

13 Turn right (W) downhill and re-cross the river at **Stokeford Bridge** in 200 metres. This was widened in 1964 but on the other side, after **Bridge Cottage** and **Nightingales Restaurant**, we have to squeeze through the railway bridge on a busy section of road.

River Avon

Hop Pole Inn

14 In 75 metres we turn left (S) into a much quieter road. Proceed through **Lower Stoke**. Pass **Limpley Stoke Station**, **Limpley Stoke Hotel**, **Hop Pole Inn** and **Limpley Stoke Post Office**. In 500 metres, in the dip after **No. 42**, turn left (SE) beside a bungalow.

15 The path goes under a railway bridge into a sylvan view of the placid Avon. Keep the river to the left and follow a terraced path beside meadows and a power line. In 900 metres we pass to the right of a sewage works into the far corner of the pasture beside the railway cutting. A farm track leads to the level-crossing at **Freshford Halt** in 300 metres. The public path goes up and over the footbridge.

16 **Station Road** takes us uphill (SW), beside **Orchard House**, to **Rose Cottage** and **Laurel House**, in 200 metres. Around the corner, in a further 150 metres, we come to a road junction facing **Temple Court** and its Bath Sun Fire Insurance wall-plate. Turn right (NW) up **Church Hill** into **Freshford**, in 100 metres, to return to the junction beside **Freshford House** and the parish church.

Freshford

8 Southstoke and Midford

A 6-mile circuit of deep-cut valleys and lengths of the Somerset Coal Canal

Building the Somerset Coal Canal in 1795 provided below-ground confirmation of surveyor William Smith's theories. They earned him the epithet 'Father of English Geology'. He had detailed 23 distinctive horizons downwards between the chalk and the coal. Friends were amazed that he could arrange random samples of fossils into the order in which they had been laid down in the ground - and repeat the same test another day for the benefit of sceptics - which led to him being known as 'Strata Smith'. That was six decades before Charles Darwin explained the concept of evolution. He might have made more out of his scientific expertise if he had not been sacked for double-dealing, arising from the purchase of the Tucking Mill at Midford, in 1799. Smith's legacy on the ground

Level: ♣ ♣ ♣
Length: 6 miles
Terrain: Liable to be extremely damp and rather strenuous.
Park & start: In **Southstoke** village by turning south from Midford Road, the B3110, at the Cross Keys on Combe Down.
Start ref.: ST 747 613
Postcode: BA2 7DS
Public transport: Bus to Southstoke.
Websites: www.ukvillages.co.uk
www.hopeandanchormidford.co.uk

is a ribbon of bridges, locks and ponds surviving from his colliery canal. The walk also encompasses the village of Southstoke and much of idyllic Combe Hay parish. The industry has gone, and so too has much of the agriculture.

Odd Down

11 12
Hignitts Farm   1 2 ■Southstoke
Fortnight Farm
8 3 4
Rowley Farm   Dismantled Railway   7 5 Midford Aqueduct
10 9 6
Cam Brook

1 Set off (E) from **St James's Church**, beside **Alderley Cottage** and the **Manor House**, down and around the corner (S). Pass the old and rambling **Packhorse Inn** and the **Village Hall** in 150 metres.

2 Then turn left (E) beside **Ivy Cottages**. The stone-walled track bends to the right in 50 metres and takes us downhill (SE) into pastures in 250 metres. Cross a stile beside a gate. Bear left through the

scrub to a stile in the valley bottom in 250 metres. Proceed straight ahead across the next field to a stile beside a stream in 75 metres. Follow the stream along the valley bottom to **Upper Midford** in 500 metres.

Southstoke Manor

3 Join the asphalt road for just 10 metres. Then turn left (N) into the field beside the barns and climb the slope straight ahead. On the top, in 100 metres, we cross a stile and then turn right. Now turn right again, across a second stile, and bear right (E) in the parkland field. Cross it to a stile beside a gate beneath horse chestnuts in 300 metres.

4 Turn right (SE) down the main road to the cross-roads in 100 metres. Turn left (NE) to the next cross-roads, between **Morgan's Forge** and the **Old Post Office** in 200 metres. Turn right (SE), downhill for 200 metres, into a view featuring the platform of former **Midford Station** and the distant but distinctive Malthouse at the Old Brewery.

Midford Aqueduct

5 Turn left (E) at the main road, under the Somerset and Dorset **Viaduct** of grey and red engineering bricks, to the **Hope and Anchor** in 50 metres. Turn immediately right (SW) beside the pub sign. A path takes us under the next railway arch and emerges in the former channel of the **Somerset Coal Canal** in 150 metres. Follow it straight ahead, to pass **Midford Aqueduct** in 200 metres and a hump-backed canal bridge in a further 150 metres. Both are in Bath stone from the Combe Down quarries. In 100 metres we turn left and then right to pass under another old railway. This one starred in *The Titfield Thunderbolt* comedy of the 1950s.

6 In 100 metres we turn left into the field on the other side and again follow the former canal towpath with **Cam Brook** across to the right. Pass remains of half-filled locks. In 600 metres we follow the canal across the next meadow towards a wooded length of railway embankment in a further 600 metres.

Engine Wood takes its name from a stationary steam engine that pumped the water over the hill for the Bull's Nose series of locks until they were immobilised by landslips and leaks in 1812.

The Wheatsheaf

(7) Turn right and then immediately left with the canal down to the left and the railway up to the right. Follow the grassy track (NW) to the road in 400 metres. Cross it and go under the railway arch. Then continue straight ahead, with the canal and its major **Bull's Nose** lock-system to the left, to a stile and gate at the end of **Engine Wood** in 500 metres.

(8) Proceed into the field for 75 metres. Then cross the stream and bear left (SW), up through the scrub, to a stile beside the beech trees at the top end of the wood in 150 metres. Bear right across this pasture to a stile tucked away in the far corner in 200 metres. Turn left on the other side, down beside the stables and through Rowley Farm, to the road in 500 metres.

From 1805-dated Midford Aqueduct the main length of the Coal Canal turned south, across the Cam Brook, to follow the Wellow Brook to Wellow, Foxcote, Writhlington, Radstock and Welton.

(9) Turn right (W) down to the next junction in 250 metres. Turn right (N), uphill between **Cam Brook Cottage** and **The Wheatsheaf**, for 100 metres. Turn left (W), above the brook and before the cemetery, and descend steps in 30 metres to a stile into the field in a further 30 metres. Turn right, for 40 metres,

Known as the Bull's Nose, sections of John Rennie's chain of 22 locks survive in a horseshoe-shaped bend on the Somerset Coal Canal in a deep cut valley at Combe Hay, from where the waterway headed for Camerton and Paulton Basin.

(10) In 400 metres we rise on to a byway below **Week Farm**. Turn right (N) to **Fortnight Farm** and the junction with the next unpaved road in 800 metres. Here we turn left, up to the road junction in the trees, in 300 metres.

Fortnight Farm

The branch railway from Limpley Stoke to Camerton, which closed on 15 February 1951, had intermediate stations at Monkton Combe, Midford Halt, Combe Hay Halt and Dulverton Colliery Halt.

across the top of the slope to a stile into scrubby woodland. The public path follows the stream for 200 metres and then joins it, literally, as we go through a culvert under the railway embankment. On the other side, in 50 metres, we continue straight ahead (NW), and keep the stream to our left for 150 metres.

Rowley

11 Turn immediately right (SE), without joining the road, into the field. Then turn right again, avoiding the track towards the school on Odd Down, along another path (E) which follows the scrub-belt to a gate and stile in 200 metres.

12 The track becomes an asphalt drive as it passes the grounds of **Sulis Manor** in 500 metres. In a further 600 metres we come to the millennium viewpoint, beside the barns of **Hignitts Farm**, with a view across Somerset to Cranmore Tower. Follow the drive (SE) down the hill for 150 metres. Then turn left (ENE) at its junction with the next drive to return to the gates into **Southstoke** in 100 metres.

The coal canal project was revived at various times, particularly in 1850, but was rendered unusable when railway navvies constructed embankments across its course - to the disappointment of boys from Downside School who used to skate along it to Bath in cold winters.

Bull's Nose Locks

9 Newton St Loe and Stanton Prior

Elegant parkland and touches of grandeur

Level: 🥾🥾
Length: 6 miles
Terrain: Plenty of straight paths, and no serious slopes, but expect a number of muddy patches.
Park & start: Turn off the A39 and A4 between Bath and Corston at Globe Inn Roundabout, and then take two right turns up into **Newton St Loe village**, to the wide street facing the gates of Holy Trinity parish church.
Start ref.: ST 701 649
Postcode: BA2 9BR
Public transport: Bus to Bath Spa University.
Websites: www.bathspa.ac.uk
www.mapsgoogle.co.uk

Cobbled pavements and a picturesque mix of Georgian elegance and rustic thatch. dignified with crests, inscriptions and date-stones, make Newton St Loe a classy historic village. Newton Park is the picturesque setting of Bath Spa University College. This is top-quality heritage landscape, having been created for Earl Temple by the master himself, Lancelot 'Capability' Brown. He formed the double lakes and a superb genuine fortress was restored into a sham-castle folly, complete with gatehouses. That had been the seat of the earlier Hungerford and Langton families. Beyond, the little village of Stanton Prior has avoided suburban implants and is still a community centred on its cows. In St Lawrence's Church, the treasure is a delightful carving of a Puritan family of the Civil War era, featuring Thomas Cox who died in 1650. Coats of arms on the ceiling of the nave are for Bath Abbey and the Hungerford family. The common touch is restricted to the porch.

New Barn 11
10
9
Weirs
College
St Loe's Castle
5
4
3
2
1
Newton Park
12 13 14
Newton St Loe
6
7
Stanton Prior

The yew tree in Stanton Prior churchyard is said to have been planted over the mass-grave of mediaeval plague victims.

1 Set off (E) along the street, away from the church gates, to pass the historic **Free Schools**. Proceed straight ahead at the junction, in 100 metres, with the **Duchy Estate Office** to your right. Fork right at the corner in a further 100 metres, to pass **The Mount**, and then turn right (SW) beside the sycamore tree and colossal flowerpot on the otherwise minuscule village green. **The Thatch**, with an oversized crest, is to the right and the **Post Office** to the left.

Newton House

2 Walk down the street (W) and pass the three thatched cottages. Turn left (SW) beside the lodge in 50 metres. This is the historic main drive into **Newton Park**. Keep the principal buildings of **Bath Spa University** to your right in 800 metres. Pass **Newton House** and **St Loe's Castle** in a further 400 metres. Behind them is a lakeland nature reserve.

Richard Jones's Free Schools at Newton St Loe have an elaborate 1698 date-panel, plus a restoration plaque for George V's coronation road of 1911.

(3) After the main car-park we pass **Newton, Corston** and **Stanton** halls of residence. Penultimately, on the south side of the campus, are **Twinhoe** and the stone-built **Old Dairy** with their parking area beyond. Finally, in 250 metres, we pass the **Sports Changing Rooms**.

Newton St Loe

(4) The public path proceeds straight ahead, across playing fields, to a stile midway along the fence on the other side in 200 metres. Optionally, you can divert into the campus by following directions on a board between the Changing Rooms and the sports fields. A permissive path passes below the castle and along the shore of both historic **Fish Ponds**. This will add a mile to the walk but is well worth the effort.

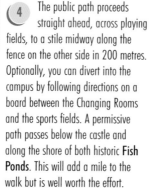

The Old Rectory is now the Duchy of Cornwall's estate office and the shield of arms of the Prince of Wales - with 15 pellets - can be seen on buildings and gates around the entire course of this walk.

(5) Our ongoing route, after crossing the playing fields, is towards the prominent church tower. Earthworks and quarry holes, the lesser features under foot, include the ancient line of the **Wansdyke**. Cross into the following field, in 300 metres, and keep a hedgerow to your right. Drop down to a stile in the far corner in 400 metres. Enter an overgrown length of green lane and follow the stream around to the left.

6 In 200 metres we turn left across a footbridge and stile into a tiny triangle of woodland. Cross the stile into the field and follow the hedgerow, towards the barns to the left of the church and village, over the site of mediaeval closes to the stile beside the gate in 250 metres.

7 Cross the road into an arable field and head for **Stanton Prior**. Our next stile is in the hedge, in 200 metres, beside a power line pole. Continue across the stony field towards the cluster of buildings to the right of the church. The stile is beside the gate at the road junction in 200 metres. **Priory Farm** is to the left.

The Wansdyke was a defensive ditch and bank forming the Dark Ages frontier — against the Anglo-Saxon advance — of legendary King Arthur's real-time period in post-Roman Britain.

8 Continue straight ahead (W), passing the **Old Rectory**, to **St Lawrence's Church**. Follow the road down the slope, and right (NE) at the corner, and also right at the junction, around to the rather grand frontage of **Poplar Farm** in 500 metres. Turn left, across the little bridge, and then right at the junction in 40 metres.

Poplar Farm

9 Follow the road (N), uphill, for 1,500 metres. Upwards and leftwards across the field is the wooded profile of Stantonbury Hill, doubly ancient with an Iron Age fort plus the Wansdyke, attached to its northern rampart. Coming level with it, at the first of its two gates, we re-cross the ploughed-out course of Wansdyke. Take your bearings from the second gate. Head towards The Wheatsheaf public house, beside the A30 on the northern skyline, but only go halfway towards it.

10 In 300 metres, beyond the dip and after the rise, turn right (E) across a stile into the field. The Wheatsheaf is now to our left. Follow the hedge, an old stone wall and a little brook, and pass **New Barn** in 900 metres.

Beyond, in 100 metres, there are two public path options in the pasture after a stile. Ours is straight ahead, following the stream, down into the valley below **South Cleve** woodland and then along the northern side of Newton Park.

In 900 metres we skirt the lower lake, keeping its fence to the right, with the outer bulwark of university buildings dominating its opposite bank. After the weir - or cascade as Capability Brown called it - we follow the fence straight ahead, up the slope, and cross the campus access road.

Puritan Cox family

The public path continues straight ahead, uphill on the other side, via an anglers' car-park. Pass through the laurels and follow a stone wall into **Newton St Loe** in 500 metres. Just after passing road-side cottages we turn left (N), up the drive, to outlying **No. 6**.

On coming level with the house in 100 metres we turn right (NE), above and to the left of its garage. A kissing gate opens into the hillside pasture. The churchyard is next, in 100 metres, with your car beyond.

St Loe's Castle

10 Kelston Park and Saltford Lock

Riverside paths and railway cycleways

Saltford was the highest point to which the sea water could flow - hence its name - and remains a scenic oasis. The ground rises into a dramatic parkland panorama with its great house at Kelston Park having been the Elizabethan home of the Harrington family, whose famous member founded the Harmonic Society. It was rebuilt in the 1850s by Lieutenant-Colonel Inigo Jones, a descendant of the architect. Across its view, a gash left by Dr Richard Beeching's railway closures might have been absorbed back into the meadows - or become another bypass - but this lost line has been put to more imaginative use. Between 1975 and 1985, the former Midland Railway track into Bath became part of a 15-mile cycleway sponsored by

Level: 🥾
Length: 7 miles
Terrain: Leisure paths across meadows, but these can flood to several feet , as in winter 2000 and the wet autumn of 2009.
Park & start: From the **A4** at **Newbridge** in the wide layby on the south side between the actual **New Bridge** and **The Boathouse**.
Start ref.: ST 717 657
Postcode: BA1 3HN
Public transport: Buses to Bristol.
Websites: www.parksandgardens.ac.uk www.sabrain.com/boathouse

Sustrans (a contraction of Sustainable Transport). It includes sculptures and seats but could do with the volunteers returning, with machetes, to provide breaks and viewpoints.

Jolly Sailor

Saltford

Lock

Tennant's Wood

River Avon

Kelston Park

New Bridge

A4

Bristol Bath Railway Path

1 Set off by crossing the road to the pavement and follow it (W), for 50 metres, across **New Bridge**. Proceed on the other side for 50 metres.

2 Turn right (N) down the steps and across the stile to the concrete road which is the towpath along the **River Avon**. The Boathouse is across the water. There is an arable field to the left, across to the site of a Roman villa, on the rise beyond the road. In 250 metres we leave the access road beside **Newton Meadow Treatment Works** and skirt its right-hand fence. Follow the path below **Kelston Park** (W), with its mistletoe-clumped limes, to the iron-girder railway bridge of the Midland Railway in 1,500 metres.

Kelston Park

3 Pass under the bridge and proceed (SW) to the real railway, the Great Western line, in 350 metres. From here the path (NW) is sandwiched between trains to the left and water to the right. Pass the boathouses and cross the footbridge at **Saltford Marina** in 2,000 metres. In 150 metres we pass the **Riverside Inn** opposite **Kelston Lock**.

4 Continue to follow the river and then turn left before the **Old Brass Mill** to emerge from a narrow path between the gardens, at **The Shallows** - a road - in 250 metres.

5 Turn right (N), to pass **Saltford Brass Mill** and walls incorporating blocks of metallic slag. Opposite the kiln of Harford and Company's brass battery works are its former workers' cottages and their 1865-dated chapel. Pass below the neat grassy slopes beside the **Swallows Pumping Station**, and the **Old Rectory**, and continue to the junction beside the **Bird-in-Hand** in 500 metres.

Duplication of railway lines gave Saltford two stations with the second being named 'Kelston for Saltford' to try and mitigate confusion (though it had no access to Kelston).

River Avon

Saltford Lock

6 Turn right (NE) into **Mead Lane**, downhill and under the old railway, and follow it to the **Avon Lane** junction in 700 metres. Bear right, passing waterfront villas in the former quarry to the left, to **Sheppard's Boatyard**.

7 Turn right, through the main gate, and then pass between two fences in 10 metres. The waterside path leads to scenic **Saltford Lock** and the Jolly Sailor in 150 metres.

The riverside path by the Avon, technically a towpath, links the navigable length of tidal estuary with the western end of the Kennet and Avon Canal.

The Boathouse – a Victorian boating station – is a living museum with boat hire facilities and a summertime service to Pulteney Bridge.

8 Retrace your steps (SW) back to the boatyard, and along Mead Lane for 600 metres, to the car-park below the Bird-in-Hand.

9 Here we climb the embankment and turn left (S) along the cycleway. Saltford Lock is now behind you, to the left, and the parish church down to the right. This was **Kelston for Saltford Station**. Cross the **River Avon** in 100 metres. **Tennant's Wood** is to the left and the embankment has also scrubbed-up on the other side.

The Pines Express from Manchester to Bournemouth used to come down the line, from Yate to Midland Bridge Road in Bath, before closure on 31 May 1971.

(10) In 2,000 metres we re-cross the river (SE) and our earlier route in the meadows below Kelston Park. In a further 1,000 metres the cycleway passes under the **A4**. Next, in another 600 metres, it again crosses the Avon, on entering the city.

En route public houses are The Boathouse beside New Bridge, the Riverside Inn at Kelston Lock, the Bird-in-Hand at Saltford, and the Jolly Sailor at Saltford Lock.

Saltford Marina

(11) Turn left (NE) to cross a foot-bridge over the entrance to **Bath Marina**. Return to **New Bridge** in 400 metres. On emerging from under it, facing **The Boathouse**, we turn right (E) and climb the steps to the pavement opposite the parking place, in 50 metres.

The Boathouse